MW01378445

the Wind

The Bob Dylan Story

Bruce T. Paddock

Boston, Massachusetts
Chandler, Arizona
Glenview, Illinois
Upper Saddle River, New Jersey

Illustrations

Opener, 1, 2, 3, 4, 5, 6, 7, 9, 10, 11, 12, 13, 14, 15 Graham Kennedy.

Photographs

Every effort has been made to secure permission and provide appropriate credit for photographic material.
The publisher deeply regrets any omission and pledges to correct errors called to its attention in subsequent editions.

Unless otherwise acknowledged, all photographs are the property of Pearson Education, Inc.

Photo locators denoted as follows: Top (T), Center (C), Bottom (B), Left (L), Right (R), Background (Bkgd)

8 National Archives, Pacific Region.

ISBN-13: 978-0-328-67727-6
ISBN-10: 0-328-67727-2

1 2 3 4 5 6 7 8 9 10 V0FL 15 14 13 12 11

A Famous Songwriter

Bob Dylan is one of the most influential songwriters in American music. He has experimented with many **genres**, such as R & B (rhythm and blues), rock and roll, pop, country, and others. Dylan doesn't just sing and play several instruments. He writes his own music, too. He helped create a type of songwriting that is personal and heartfelt. The words to his songs have been analyzed by fans and music **critics** alike.

Dylan first made a name for himself in the 1960s with a style called folk music. Many folk fans were not pleased when one of their favorite performers then moved on to different kinds of music, but Dylan didn't mind the criticism. He felt he needed to try new styles to be creative. Over the last fifty years, he has helped invent new types of musical styles, such as country rock. His songwriting style has had an impact on thousands of singer-songwriters who have come after him.

The Early Years

Robert Zimmerman was born on May 24, 1941, in Duluth, Minnesota. People called him "Bobby." When he was six years old, his family moved to a small town called Hibbing, Minnesota. Bobby Zimmerman, his brother David, and their parents lived in a middle-class neighborhood. Theirs was one of the few Jewish families in Hibbing.

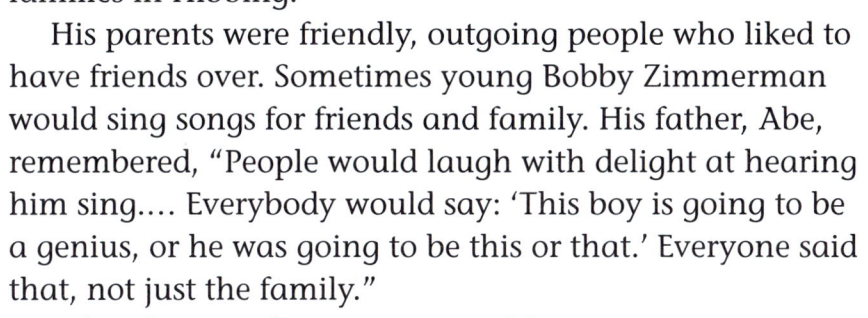

His parents were friendly, outgoing people who liked to have friends over. Sometimes young Bobby Zimmerman would sing songs for friends and family. His father, Abe, remembered, "People would laugh with delight at hearing him sing.... Everybody would say: 'This boy is going to be a genius, or he was going to be this or that.' Everyone said that, not just the family."

When he was about ten years old, young Zimmerman started spending a lot of time alone in his room, writing poetry. In junior high school, he became interested in music and decided to take up an instrument. After trying and failing with the trumpet, the saxophone, and several other instruments, he turned to the guitar. He taught himself to play by reading from a manual. Soon, his guitar was a constant companion. Wherever he went, he always had his guitar slung over his back.

In high school, Bobby Zimmerman's interest in music kept growing. He began writing his own music and learned how to play the harmonica and the piano. He was also amazed by a new style of music that was just becoming popular—rock and roll. Bobby's favorite rockers were Elvis Presley and Little Richard.

Little Richard

At this time, young Zimmerman still spent much of his time by himself, but he also had a drive to perform his music. He and his high school friends formed different bands, with names such as the Golden Chords and Elston Gunn and His Rock Boppers. Music seemed to bring Zimmerman out of his shell. He would even imitate the showy rocker Little Richard when he and his band played at high school dances.

In 1959, Zimmerman went to the University of Minnesota in Minneapolis to study art. More importantly, though, he grew as a musician. He started listening to blues music and spending time with folk musicians. Zimmerman loved the messages he heard in folk music. The music was often about struggle and hardship but was hopeful at the same time. His favorite folk musician was Woody Guthrie, who had written well-known songs such as "This Land Is Your Land." Zimmerman started performing folk music using a new name—Bob Dylan. He changed his name in honor of the great Welsh poet Dylan Thomas.

Moving to New York

During the summer after his freshman year of college, Dylan went to Denver, Colorado. There he met a blues musician named Jesse Fuller. Fuller inspired Dylan's decision to start performing with a harmonica rack. The rack, resting on his shoulders, allowed Dylan to play the harmonica while keeping his hands free to play the guitar at the same time. This became Dylan's well-known performance style.

Dylan returned to the University of Minnesota in the fall, but he was becoming restless. In January 1961, he dropped out of school and moved to New York City. Part of the reason he wanted to go to New York was to visit his hero, Woody Guthrie. Guthrie was being treated for severe health problems there.

New York had an exciting folk music scene. It was centered on a number of clubs and coffeehouses in a neighborhood called Greenwich Village. Dylan performed there, and impressed just about everyone who heard him. He also wrote songs at an astonishing rate.

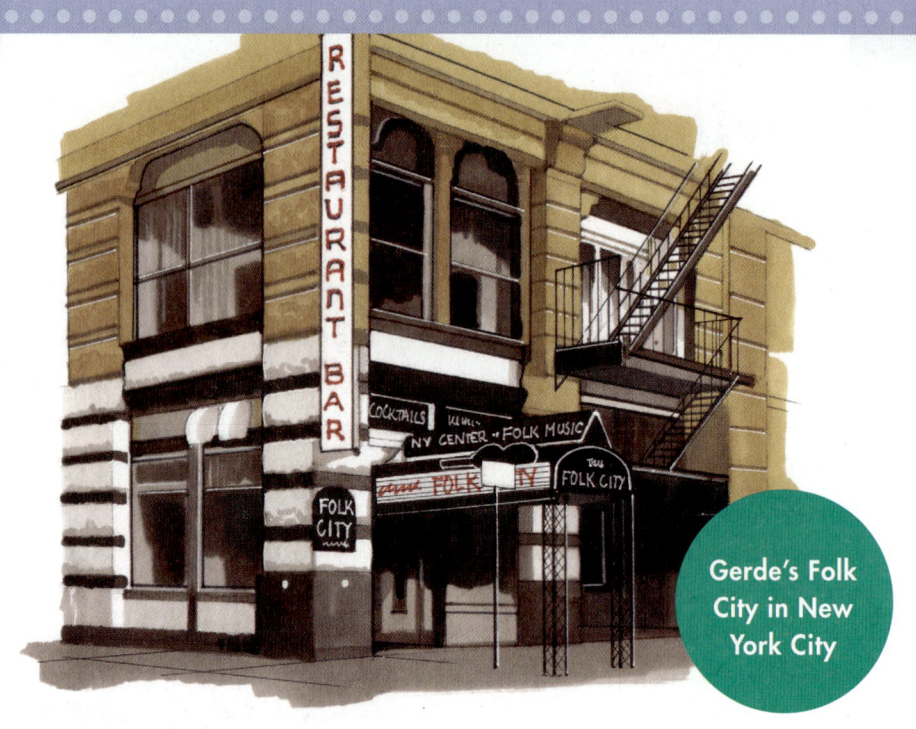

Gerde's Folk City in New York City

A Record Deal

In the fall of 1961, a writer happened to be at one of Dylan's performances in a New York City club called Gerde's Folk City. Soon after, an article praising Dylan's talent appeared in the newspaper *The New York Times*. Based on that article, a record company, Columbia Records, sought out Dylan. The company offered him a contract to write and record albums. Dylan agreed.

When Columbia signed Dylan, the company wanted the public to learn more about him so people would become interested in hearing his music. The company's head of **publicity** asked Dylan questions about his life, but Dylan didn't like answering personal questions. He gave few straight answers. This interview was a sign of things to come. Dylan never liked answering questions from the **press**.

Becoming a Star

Dylan's first album for Columbia Records, titled *Bob Dylan*, was released in 1962. It had only two original songs written by Dylan. The rest were **covers** of folk and blues songs. His next album, *The Freewheelin' Bob Dylan*, came out in 1963. *Freewheeling* means wild, or not under control. Dylan wrote most of the songs on this album himself.

Freewheelin' was much more popular than Dylan's first album. Fans loved Dylan's unusual raspy voice, as well as the nonviolent message in his music. At the time, many Americans were protesting the United States' involvement in the Vietnam War. Many also worked to help African Americans gain more **civil rights**. Several folk songs of the 1960s became symbols of the civil rights and antiwar movements. One of these songs was "Blowin' in the Wind," from Dylan's *Freewheelin'* album. The song seemed to question how many deaths it would take before the war was over. Another song from the same album, "Masters of War," was a protest against the arms race between the United States and its rival, the Soviet Union.

With *Freewheelin'*, Dylan became a big star. He also began influencing fellow musicians. The group Peter, Paul and Mary covered the song "Blowin' in the Wind." Their version became a huge hit on the pop music charts.

Dylan's next album, *The Times They Are A-Changin'*, established him as a leading folk performer. It didn't hurt that he was dating Joan Baez, who was considered the top woman star of American folk music. Theirs was a professional as well as a personal partnership. Dylan wrote some of Baez's biggest hits, and she introduced him to thousands of new fans when she invited him to play at her concerts.

Joan Baez and Bob Dylan

NEWPORT FOLK FESTIVAL

Dylan was booed when he played rock songs with an electric guitar at the Newport Folk Festival in 1965.

The Rock Years

By 1964, Dylan was playing about 200 concerts per year, but he was becoming tired of writing and singing only folk music. He wanted to explore other forms of music and to write more personal songs, not just songs about political issues. In the summer of 1964, Dylan released *Another Side of Bob Dylan*, and the songs on this album leaned more toward blues and rhythm and blues than folk. His next album, *Bringing It All Back Home*, was released in March 1965. It showed heavy rock influences. Some of the songs were acoustic, but the rest were electric and loud.

Rock fans ate up the new sound, but Dylan's folk music fans felt betrayed. On July 25, 1965, Dylan performed some of his new rock songs at a folk music festival in Newport, Rhode Island. He was joined by a large backup band, and instead of using an **acoustic** guitar as folk musicians did, he played an electric guitar. The audience, filled with folk music fans, booed Dylan.

The Beatles were the biggest rock band of the 1960s.

The festival in Newport wasn't the only concert where folk fans reacted poorly to Dylan's new sound, but he never took it personally. He continued to write rock songs. Over time, he gained even more fans.

In August 1965, Dylan released an album with a rock and pop flavor called *Highway 61 Revisited*. This was probably his most **innovative** period. The album included the now-classic song "Like a Rolling Stone." Most songwriters of the time kept their songs under three minutes, but Dylan broke with this tradition when he extended "Like a Rolling Stone" to six minutes. The song rose to number two on the music charts and remains one of Dylan's best-known songs.

Dylan also continued to inspire other musicians. Between 1964 and 1966, his songs were covered by more than a hundred other performers, including bands like the Byrds and the Turtles. The famous British group, the Beatles, cited him as an influence when they turned to writing more **introspective**, personal songs in the late 1960s.

Another New Direction

Dylan had never been the most outgoing person, but he played a lot of concerts and was a very public figure by the mid-1960s. That changed on July 29, 1966 when Dylan crashed his motorcycle near his home in Woodstock, New York. He suffered serious injuries to his head and neck and almost died. For more than a year, he disappeared from the public eye while he recovered.

Dylan spent much of his recovery time with his wife, Sara, and their children. Eventually, he turned back to music. He rented a house in nearby West Saugerties, New York, with his backup band the Hawks. Dylan spent months playing and recording new music. In December 1967, he released *John Wesley Harding*, which had a mellow country sound. It surprised audiences and was a big hit in both the United States and Britain. This album, as well as his next one, *Nashville Skyline*, helped create the country rock genre.

Soon after *Harding* came out, Dylan started to make public appearances again. His first performance after his accident was in New York City in January 1968. Dylan played at a **memorial** concert for his hero Woody Guthrie, who had recently died.

Dylan on his motorcycle in 1965, before his accident

The 1970s and 1980s

In the early 1970s, Dylan turned to other creative activities besides music. He published the book *Tarantula* in 1971. It was a collection of unconnected writings and was not received well by the public. Two years later, he acted in a film called *Pat Garrett and Billy the Kid* and wrote the **soundtrack** for the movie as well. The soundtrack sold well. It included another now-classic Dylan song, "Knockin' on Heaven's Door." The song has been covered by many artists, including the heavy metal band Guns N' Roses.

Dylan found more success in 1974 with *Planet Waves*, his first album to reach number one on the music charts. That year, he started his first tour in eight years. The tour sold out nationwide and became one of the most successful rock and roll tours in history.

In the mid-1970s, Dylan returned to his folk roots. He went back to Greenwich Village and played in clubs with his old folk musician friends. The folk music scene was smaller than it had been in the early 1960s but was still active. Starting in 1975, Dylan spent a year touring with some of the biggest names in folk music—Joni Mitchell, Joan Baez, and others. The tour was called The Rolling Thunder Revue.

Bob Dylan (far right) with other artists in the Rolling Thunder Revue tour

A Grammy Award looks like a small gramophone, a device used to play recorded music long ago.

In 1978, Dylan took another unexpected turn. He announced he had become a Christian, and the following year he released an album of Christian music called *Slow Train Coming*. The album had a rock sound with religious lyrics.

Audiences and music critics were again surprised by this turn, but the album was popular. It peaked at number three on the music charts and won Dylan his first Grammy, an award that recognizes achievements in the music industry. The Grammy was for Best Rock Vocal Performance, Male. After two more religious albums that were poorly reviewed and didn't sell well, Dylan returned to nonreligious music.

In the 1980s, Dylan released several more albums of various music genres—blues, rock, folk, and even dance music. He also toured with the rock groups Tom Petty and the Heartbreakers, and with the Grateful Dead. In 1988, Dylan teamed up with four other well-known musicians to briefly form a band and record two albums. This "supergroup," called the Traveling Wilburys, included four of Dylan's friends, Tom Petty, Jeff Lynne, Roy Orbison, and George Harrison, who had been in the Beatles.

A Comeback

In the 1990s, Dylan put out many albums. Several of them were collections of his greatest hits, not new songs. Some critics said that Dylan's best work was behind him and he would no longer create great original music. Dylan silenced the critics when he released *Time Out of Mind* in 1997. The album became a hit and got good reviews. It won three Grammy Awards,

Dylan accepting his Album of the Year Grammy for Time Out of Mind

including Album of the Year. The other two awards were in the folk and rock categories, showing how hard it is to place Dylan in any one category.

There was no doubt that Dylan was back. In 2000, he wrote the song "Things Have Changed" for the movie *Wonder Boys*. He won an Academy Award, or Oscar, for Best Original Song. His 2006 album *Modern Times* went platinum, meaning it sold at least one million copies. And just to keep his fans guessing, one of his most recent albums, released in 2009, was a collection of Christmas songs.

A Living Legend

Today Bob Dylan is considered not just one of the greatest musicians of his generation, but one of the greatest American songwriters ever. He has recorded dozens of albums, sold millions of copies, and continues to perform and record. His creative songwriting and many musical styles have inspired countless other musicians. More than 2,000 artists have recorded hundreds of his songs.

Dylan has won numerous awards for his work. In 1997, he received Kennedy Center Honors, the highest award for artistic excellence in the United States. He was the first rock star to be honored in this way. When Dylan was **inducted** into the Rock and Roll Hall of Fame in 1988, rocker Bruce Springsteen spoke in Dylan's honor. Springsteen said,

"He invented a new way a pop singer could sound. He broke through the limitations of what a recording artist could achieve, and he changed the face of rock and roll forever and ever."

Dylan performed at the 2011 Grammys with the bands Mumford and Sons and the Avett Brothers.

Glossary

acoustic relating to a type of music that is produced by nonelectric instruments

civil rights the rights of citizens

cover in music, to record a song that has been written and recorded by someone else first

critic a person who writes reviews judging an art form, such as music

genre a particular type of music or literature

induct to bring in as a member

innovative doing something new and different

introspective looking inward to examine one's own thoughts and feelings

memorial something done in memory of a person who has died

press companies and people who report and publish the news, such as newspapers, magazines, and reporters

publicity activities to make someone or something known to the public

soundtrack the music that accompanies a movie